Suddenly Saved, Single and Parenting

Sharon C. B. Hunter

Edited by: Claude R. Royston

BK Royston Publishing, LLC
Jeffersonville, IN

BK Royston Publishing
P. O. Box 4321
Jeffersonville, IN 47131
502-802-5385
http://bkroystonpublishing.com
bkroystonpublishing@gmail.com

© Copyright – 2016

All Rights Reserved. No part of this book may be reproduced, stored in a retrieval system, or transmitted by any means without the written permission of the author.

Cover Design: Bill Lacy

ISBN-13: 978-0692666074

ISBN-10: 0692666079

LCCN: 2016904198

Dedication

This book is dedicated to all the single parents. Although you may not have seen your life as a single parent, God promises never to leave you alone. I am praying for you, and this book intends to give you some new perspectives about life as a saved and single parent.

Acknowledgements

After the failure of my first marriage, I was extremely hurt, and I had the dating skills of a 15 year old girl. However, God saw fit to lead me to a loving church filled with loving people that helped me grow in my walk with God. The different ministries of the church helped me to develop as a Woman of God and I will never forget it.

There is a Scripture in the Bible that says, "....Children are a gift from the Lord; they are a reward from him... " (Psalm 127:3 New Living Translation).

I am so grateful that God was persistent with me and did not quit until I was able to see my children as gifts, blessings, and rewards that He gave me. God showed me how to open, cherish, maintain, and love the gifts He gave me in the form of my children. The reward I have found in their smiles, wisdom, love and joy is priceless and continues to bless my life. I am also thankful that my children accepted my apologies when I missed the mark. They forgave me when I was wrong as a parent, and they loved me through the good and bad times.

I bless God that He entrusted me with you, and I love you.

I want to acknowledge several women of God that helped me beyond measure. My deceased mother, Minister Mary Cummins. She believed in me, consoled me when my feelings were hurt, and pushed me when I wanted to sulk. Words will never express all that I learned from you as a mother and a minister. Elder Alice Jackson and Pastor Charmaine Flanagan although we did not get to talk every day, the wisdom God gave each of you impacted my life forever. Pastor Roz Daugherty was not afraid to share with me the pitfalls of ministry, and how to stay focused on God, my children, and my new walk.

I would also like to acknowledge Pastor James H Anderson and Apostle Derrick Flanagan. God allowed you both to help and teach me in different ways.

Also I would like to thank God for allowing me to develop life- long friendships with Crystal, my cousin, Monica, Stacy, Dana, Shawn, Steve, and Walter. These were people that listened to me when I needed to be heard, encouraged me when I felt discouraged, and introduced me to Sunday night roller skating that made all my troubles go away for a few hours.

Lastly I want to thank my husband and Pastor, Senior Pastor Dominic Hunter. I feel the love you have for me every time you give me room to be who God created me to be. Every man does not possess this gift nor do they want it. I love you and I appreciate your awesomeness in God.

I cannot mention all of the people that ministered to me, but God allows me to reflect and celebrate my new beginning in Jesus Christ that continues to overflow.

Table of Contents

Dedication
Acknowledgements
Introduction

Chapter 1	Tentacles of Bad Choices	1
Chapter 2	The Timing of Salvation and Divine Detours	9
Chapter 3	Becoming a Commercial for God	17
Chapter 4	Lessons Learned	23
Chapter 5	Four Models of Single Parents	29
Chapter 6	The Dynamics of Influence	37
Chapter 7	The Freedom of Forgiveness versus the Imprisonment of Unforgiveness	45
Chapter 8	Developing a Prayer Life	49
Chapter 9	Each Path is Different	53
Chapter 10	Sex	59

Chapter 11	It's Complicated	65
Chapter 12	Looking to the Right Source	69
About the Author		73

Introduction

There is a saying that God gave me that describes my Christian journey, "I have been in bondage and I have been free, and I like freedom so much better!" However, getting to this freedom or liberty required some work. And the truth is, after I made the decision 'to put the work in", follow God, and allow Him to teach me, I discovered it challenged me. I believe that if we are real with God, ourselves, and others we will find deliverance. However, I must admit I did not like my new challenges as a single person or a parent but I wanted to be delivered to abundant living that God had freely given.

I spent a lot of years seeking abundant living without God's influence. However, once I understood that the abundant living I longed for was not tied to a bigger home, faster car, or even more money. God desired to teach me that abundant living included His joy, peace, hope, kindness and many other fruit of the spirit that the world could never take away.

None of us are perfect and all of us have life circumstances that weigh us down. However, God wants to show us how to lay aside the weight of life and sin that distract us. What we choose to give up that is not benefiting our lives or our children's lives, He replaces with a new life that has Jesus at the foundation, a new attitude and mind in Jesus Christ, and a new season of grace and favor.

Although there are inserts of my personal journey to God, abundant living, and single parenting, this book is for anybody that wants a Godly perspective of living saved, single, and parenting.

After reading this book, I pray that you go forward on your new journey of being suddenly saved, single, and parenting with God, accepting the change, and receiving the new thing He is doing in you!

Suddenly Saved, Single and Parenting

Chapter 1

The Tentacles of Bad Choices

Finally, my brethren, be strong in the Lord, and in the power of his might. Ephesians 6:11 - Put on the whole armour of God, that ye may be able to stand against the wiles of the devil. Ephesians 6:12 - For we wrestle not against flesh and blood, but against principalities, against powers, against the rulers of the darkness of this world, against spiritual wickedness in high places.

Ephesians 6:10

    I suppose the first thought to get out of the way is, as you prepare to read this book, please remember this read will not give you every answer to every question you ever had about being a single parent. However, it is intended to be a book that may give you some insight about how to survive being saved, single, and a single parent. The goal is to assist you in learning to trust God to keep your family together, keeping your self-respect while being a single parent, and keeping sight of what kind of parent you are and want to become. Now, the second undisputable thought is, everybody has some sort of life episode that leaves you saying, "Wow, I did not see that coming!" However, the way we deal with the life episodes may vary from one person to the next. This book is about how I responded to being suddenly saved, single and single parenting. And believe it or not, it was in that order. God saved my soul through Jesus Christ. It was my chance to take, and my choice to make, so I chose Jesus. Now, I hope that does not stop you from reading this book because my core change had its roots wrapped around the anchor called Jesus! It was the teachings of the Bible that helped me to raise my children in Christ and it made the difference. One final opening statement is I must forewarn you, I write what I think, so truthfully, I really don't care if you put this book down because of Jesus. But I would hate that you miss out on some awesome insight and knowledge that may help you, challenge you, and change your way of life for the better. Because my experiences were so life changing, it is my heart's desire as we share some time with one another that you see your circumstances as opportunities instead of obstacles. It's all about perspective! However, on this journey of being suddenly, saved, single and parenting I have learned some things that may help you avoid some of the tentacles of bad choices that pull us and our children over to crazy living.

When I think of bad choices I think of an imaginary beast that looks like an Octopus. It has eight tentacles that will strong arm you into potentially deadly situations. The suckers on the underside of this beast are called BAD CHOICES, and they will suck the life out and cast you in the deepest portion of the ocean. The Beast of BAD CHOICES uses its tentacles to search, pull apart, and devour its prey. If left unattended, this Beast will take over! Does this sound dramatic? Well that is exactly how our bad choices look as they dominate our lives, if we don't get it together! Now the reality is that we all have had to deal with the BAD CHOICE Beast because we have all made a bad choice or two, three, four. You get the picture. And I am not afraid to admit, I have had my share of bad choices. I am also not afraid to admit I have made some bad choices that left me stuck on stupid. Let me also say this, I will not name all my many bad choices because that would take all day. However, if I had to pick my personal number one bad choice that sucked the life out of me was looking, thinking and wanting my life to look like somebody else's and trying to get there on my own. I would look at my friend's lives, what I saw in the magazines, on T.V., and in my head. I would decide that they had it better than me! I spent countless hours trying to make my life look flawless and do everything by myself because this is what I thought was living. However, my mother used to say all the time, 'all that glitters is not gold and all that is said is not told'. So all the effort I put into looking at the SHINE of other people's lives and thinking they had it better because of things they had, only upset me. The imitation shine did not tell the whole story. So what seemed like people able to do everything on their own was artificial. The Word of God says, in Ephesians 6:10 *Finally, my brethren, be strong in the Lord, and in the power of his might. Ephesians 6:11 Put on the whole armour of God, that ye may be able to stand against the wiles of the* devil. One the reasons I had such a hard time with this particular bad choice was, I only wanted to be strong in my own strength and not the strength of the Lord. I tried too hard to do it all by myself. I suppose to some of my family and friends I looked like the five year old that was learning to tie their shoes. Even though the child is learning how to tie their shoes, they believe they already know how to do it. So then when someone tries to teach them a better way to accomplish their goal, of tying shoes, they get all flustered, pout, and sometimes even quit. The task for the child was so much harder all because they said and believed, 'I can do it by myself'. Beloved before we move further we also have to understand there is a difference between 'I can do it by myself' which implicates that you may be trying to do something alone instead of accepting some help. On the other hand, 'I can do bad all by myself' is another sentiment that implies you are carrying someone that could help but won't. This is a totally different scenario that we will explore later. In this case, the tentacles of the Beast of bad choices seems to always toss us head first into the imaginary lake of 'dumb ideas'. It takes God to prove to us that His might and will is much better than our own. The Bible so says, in Ephesians 6:12 For we wrestle not *against flesh and blood, but against principalities, against powers, against the rulers of the darkness of this world, against spiritual wickedness in high places.* So I was wrestling with my flesh to do everything on my own, but I was also wrestling with was a controlling spirit that could not function unless it had full control of the situation. I was wrestling with myself to do IT MY WAY because I trusted me. My way was the best way. So I struggled with any authority that challenged my way. To the naked eye, it looked like I was a control freak. My flesh revealed what they saw. I did not like to do things spontaneous. I liked to know exactly what needed to be said. I would get nervous if I had not spent an exhausting amount of time thinking out different scenarios. These are some of the things people would see. The root of my bad choices was lack of faith. Which is a spirit in a high place. Lack of faith means I walked in unbelief and that did not please God. When we think of wickedness we see the big three; sex, drugs, and power. And these three are real. However, there are other vices that also cultivate wickedness. The definition of a vice is, a bad or immoral behavior or habits; a moral flaw or weakness. So then, I had a list of horrible habits that did not come from the character of God. A few heavy hitters on my list was lack of faith that lead to envy, that cultivated selfish ambition and rested in jealousy when my plans did not work. The list goes on, however, I do not stand by myself. We all have horrible habits that do not exhibit the charter of God but highlight the character of satan. Wicked ideas, wicked choices, and wicked actions that are grown and cultivated in wickedness. If left to grow without the guidance of God, the wickedness takes root, and can manipulate a person to desire only to satisfy the flesh. Part of mankind's problem is we look at the surface of our problems and think we are at the root. And just like a weed in a garden, when you pull the weed from the top soil without getting to the roots, you will see the weed again. So then, whatever problems we have that continue to exist is because it was not removed at the root. For me, the constant need to do things my own way took root and developed into disobedience. Which is rebellion. As God gave instruction, I did not want to listen. So then, my over-all life experiences were harder because I thought I had to be strong on my own, in control, and doing everything my own way. But when I think about the mantra of my time it was I can be a SUPERWOMAN. Anyone that did not have VISIBLE SUPERWOMAN status, was less than a real woman. In other words, she had a fancy job or business, a huge home or car, in essence visible things that showed she was living large. I even remember a perfume commercial that had a woman singing. The song said, "...I can bring home the bacon fry it up in a pan... I can work till 5 o'clock come home and read tickety tock...." The slogan for the perfume was, "For the 24 hour woman." I was young and impressionable, so I believed this is what it took to become a success. The Word of God said, "I can do all things THROUGH Christ who strengthens me… " However, the picture the world painted was a real woman could do everything. I did not get free from this way of thinking until my life was truly turned over to Christ Jesus. When I decided to receive God, I became stronger. When I decided to follow God, I was released from self-shame, I became wiser. My dependence on God and His power and might became easier. Transparency can be an asset in our lives. It can help you and others overcome weaknesses. When we are not afraid to tell about the things that have happened in our lives, it can help others become stronger, better and wiser. There are many single parents, like myself, that feel they have no help. God wants to show you a better way of living. You can depend on God to step in and lead you and your family in the right direction. Therefore continuing to approach life with an 'I can do it by myself' attitude does not help you or your children. The Bible says in Joshua 24: 15 "...But if serving the LORD seems undesirable to you, then choose for yourselves this day whom you will serve, whether the gods your ancestors served beyond the Euphrates, or the gods of the Amorites, in whose land you are living. But as for me and my household, we will serve the LORD." I am sure there are some that find serving God is undesirable. They love living for the gods of this time. Just like the people in Joshua 24, they have choose to chase, their own way of living, money, women, men, drugs, selfish pleasure, selfish ambition. It is a rolling list of selfish choices that have not changed. However, God gave us the right to choose. God gave us the right to decide what we want to do. I choose to listen to God and obey. I choose to leave the bondage of my bad choices. I choose to live for God because I know He teaches us to make better choices. I choose to teach my children how to live for the Lord. I chose to share some knowledge that I learned with other single parents to help them. I have had a chance to live in bondage to my bad choices and I have had a chance to live free with God and I love freedom so much better!

The Timing of Salvation
Chapter 2

For by grace you have been saved through faith. And this is not your own doing; it is the gift of God, not a result of works, so that no one may boast. 2 Corinthians 3: 17 Now the Lord is that Spirit: and where the Spirit of the Lord is, there is liberty. Ephesians 2:8-9

   It is often said that God may not come when you want Him but He will be there, right on time. So then it is safe to say that, the timing of the God is never when we think it should be. As a matter of fact, it can become almost comical the times we expected God to show up and He did not. But when He did show up, it is perfect timing! So then it is important to recognize the timing of Salvation may never fit our plans for better living, but Salvation will lead us to abundant living. And, I believe that all of us want abundant living according to how we see our lives. The bondage that I previously spoke of thrives because in our mind, we see what we want. A husband, wife, career, children and to be a great success. This is typically what people think of as better living. And just like most people, I wanted it. I had my own way of how I was going to "get to this place " The problem was my plan for better living was not the best plan and a miserable fail. The path that I had choose for myself, did not line up with God's master plan. Therefore I got all tangled up in the tentacles of my own bad choices because of bad thoughts, choices and plans. And beloved when we do not line up with God, it is destined to fail. One of the greatest human misunderstandings is, we look at failure all wrong. We see it as black and white. You failed. You're done. However, instead of seeing failure as final, why not seek to find out where you failed , why you failed, what did you miss that could have fixed the failure, What did you learn from the failure and most important, when will you re-try this failure. God wants to show us that there can be favor *in the failure.* Grace is the favor of God that I cannot achieve by getting gold stars when I do well, nor by crossing the "t's" or dotting the "I's". Grace is there when we overcome or succumb to the sin.

    For all the visual folks, look at it like this: Overcome GRACE Succumb GRACE - If we overcome a sin, Grace was there to support you. However if you failed that same Grace was there to cover you. And this had nothing to do with me or you, it was and still is a gift. The best that you and I can do is say, Thank You Lord Jesus! Thank you for blessing me. Thank you for helping me in spite of every sin you knew that I would commit along the way. Thank you Jesus for knowing the root of who I was as well as who I was not but still blessing. God has faith that we are going to get better. The above text is discussing the salvation process. It reminds the believer that Salvation is not something you can do on you own. It is a gift. Therefore no amount of work will ever give us the right to boast that we did something special.

Grace is the favor of God that supports the believer right now and in future endeavors. We need God's grace. We need God's unmerited favor to remind us He is there and we need Him. The work I thought that I must do to acquire some status with God could never be earned on my own. I had to accept the failure to help me understand the favor that God gave me. And the beauty that we cannot overlook is, God gave us the Grace that had to be served with the Salvation. The gift of salvation is given in the midst of our failures and sin because God recognizes our need and His love for us. We who are the saved received the favor of God, His Grace, to overcome the failure of sin. And although the timing of salvation in our lives seems to come at the worst possible moment, it is always the best possible moment because our plans don't work without God's grace. To use myself as an example, my plan was a happy marriage, but I had one failed marriage. My plan was to get my Bachelor's Degree, but I flunked out my freshman year. My plan was to have children after marriage, but I had my first child before I married their dad. I failed, and my strategy was so weak that this failure ruined my plans and had me walking in defeat. And whenever failure shows up, the enemy has a way of sending his two goons called defeat and depression. I felt defeat choking the hope out of my life and that lead to depression. As single parents, we have to know that depression is real. When life throws curve balls, it can get hard and depressing. However, God wanted to show us how Salvation through Christ

Jesus is the salvation for abundant living. When we accept Jesus as our Savior we begin the process of freedom. The Word of God says, 2 Corinthians 3: 17 Now the Lord is that Spirit: and where the Spirit of the Lord is, there is liberty." So our acceptance of Christ in our lives lead to Freedom. And yes that freedom introduces us to a life of possibilities including the chance to fail. However failure introduces us to grace and favor. The liberty we find in a simply failing experience helps us to receive God's assistance. God has a way of allowing the failure to happen but at the same time providing a way of escape that you know it was Him. (1 Corinthians 10:13) So again, no one can boast like they knew what they were doing. God is going to take care of it and take care of you and me. His timing is impeccable.

A Divine Detour

Romans 8:28 And we know that all things work together for good to them that love God, to them who are the called according to his purpose.

Although God's timing cannot be beat it can cause our lives to change direction. God's timing can create Divine Detours. A Divine Detour is a place that God re-directs. When God intervenes and re-directs our lives, it creates a detour. The detour takes sometimes the longest or shortest route to our destinations. However, there is something about a Divine Detour that once you get to your destination you know that the detour was the best way to go. Unfortunately our flesh gets in the way and we fight God's Divine Detours because we do not understand the detours. However a Divine Detour can bring help to our lives because it hides us from people, places, and things that mean us harm. A great Biblical story about a Divine Detour was the wise men, Joseph, Mary, and the Baby Jesus. God had warned the wise men or Magi to return to their country by another route. (Matthew 2:12) Also the Lord appeared to Joseph in a dream and advised him to "get up, Take the child and his mother, Mary and escape to Egypt...." (Matthew 2:13) When we experience Salvation, the compass that is guiding our life can change direction. So then, the Wise men lives changed when they encountered the baby Jesus, the Salvation. The Bible states God advised them to go another route. We cannot be afraid to follow God's direction when there is a change of plan. When God leads us through another route it will change and save our lives. Whenever we encounter Jesus Christ, our lives will change. My Grandmother use to say, "He will either DRAW you or DRIVE you..." it is still our choice! Jesus is a gentleman therefore He does not force us to follow Him. The parents of Jesus, Joseph and Mary, lives changed when Jesus, the Salvation, entered their lives. God told Joseph to get up and go to Egypt, and the Holy Spirit encountered Mary to let her know that she was the chosen vessel to birth our Jesus. The point God makes to us is these Divine Detours ultimately carry the power to bless us beyond measure. However, the key to receiving these blessings is obedience. Our Biblical example shows the Magi, Joseph, and Mary were obedient. The Magi received a warning in a dream, and they obeyed. The Lord appeared to Joseph in a dream and provided him with specific instruction as to how to protect the life of the Baby Jesus and His Mother, Mary. He obeyed. Mary accepted the will of God that ultimately created a detour from tradition. She obeyed. The Divine Detour for the Magi, Joseph and Mary was a part of the ALL THINGS Working Together for the good. Now the reality is it does not always feel like it is working together. However beloved, we must not trust our feelings alone because they lie like an old dog on the porch of a hot summer day. Our feelings cannot be trusted because those feelings can lead us to things that are not true. Your feelings will say, 'I love him', but it's really your body saying, 'I crave him' your feelings will say, 'I can't stand her', but what you really mean is you can't stand yourself. Since I made the choice to love Jesus, I trust that ALL of IT will work out for my good. Therefore a divine detour will lead us to our destiny. We experience ABUNDANT LIVING when we get to the destination of our Divine Detour. It was necessary for God to lead the Magi, Mary, Joseph, and Jesus on another route because their lives depended on it. And since their lives touched other lives through Salvation, we depended on them to be obedient to the will of God. Their obedience led to abundant living for all those who believe in Jesus Christ. *So then, all things working together for the good (Romans* 8:28) does not mean that everything that happened to you and I was good. To be honest, some of the stuff that happened to you and I was very bad. However when we are obedient and follow God no matter where He leads, we cannot lose! We have to continue to tell ourselves, 'with God I cannot lose!' God has a way of taking a bad situation and helping us find the good and how it all works together. However, we have to believe God can do it. Another problem we all face some time or another is that we all become guilty of focusing on the detours. For me, I became broken-hearted, bitter and distracted when my dreams of abundant living seemed to disintegrate. So instead of focusing on the deeper blessings of how God gave me favor in the failure that helped me keep my children and my mind. I focused on the topical distractions of the husband that left. The life that my friends had but I did not. The desire to have my children grow up in a ginormous home, equipped with a pool, big back yard, and the finest of schools and clothing. These distractions were debilitating. The distractions made me weak and hindered my Salvation process. These debilitating distractions made me bitter. I was bitter about other women that were horrible to their husbands, yet they still had a husband and mine was gone. I was bitter that I had four children to raise on my own. I felt that I had failed my babies in my choice to marry their dad. And I was most certainly bitter about living out of one room in my parents' house with my parents, my two youngest sisters and my four children. At rock bottom,

I had purchased a new garbage can and place five people clothing down in the can. I put it in the closet of my childhood bedroom. This room was now the home of my little family. The Divine Detour seemed hopeless. And even though I had accepted Christ, I still was working out my soul salvation in fear and trembling (Philippians 2:12). I was scared that even though I had Jesus, this seemingly hopeless place was going to be my life, forever. My hopes of making it to my divine destination of abundant living would never come to pass by the way my life looked. God in His infinite beauty and wisdom desires for mankind to look beyond the way things seem. These distractions have a way of hindering our journey. God likes to use situations to help us grow stronger as we journey with Him. So then God helped me to focus on Him and not the distractions that were there to debilitate me. So my life suddenly detoured into Salvation, single living, and single parenting. Many times single parent's lives detour to destinations that feel hopeless. Do not allow this hopelessness to define you. When we allow these troublesome moments to define our lives we can become consumed with self-hate, defeat, and an overall misconception of who God is calling us to become. Remember there is a plan that is going to bless you and your children. Over time with the help of God, we learn to become who He is calling us to be. We learn to become willing and obedient. (Isaiah 1:19) We make choices to allow God to show us how all the Divine Detours can work out for our good. (Romans 8:28). 26

Becoming a Commercial for God
Chapter 3

Also I heard the voice of the Lord, saying, Whom shall I send, and who will go for us? Then said I, Here am I; send me.   Isaiah 6:8

      A commercial is one of the top advertising strategies for any company to get their business before the public. As the commercial promotes the product, the people that watch the commercial decide if they are going to buy it. My heart said, 'I want to be a commercial for God.' However, my head took some time to catch up with what that statement really meant. When I first accepted Christ in my life, I was on a business trip to Atlanta, Georgia. My mother and I were going to start a beauty supply store. This was our plan. The entire trip was almost canceled because we didn't have enough money to go. However, the Lord provided enough money to go and take my grandmother Earlene Jones. She was saved, sanctified and filled with the Holy Ghost. My mother Mary Cummins, at that time, loved God but was a little farther from the Lord. She, like most of us, was still interested in doing the things she liked. God used the trip to save me and bring her back closer to Him. My friend from high school had recently gotten married to a very good Christian man. Over the years, we kept up with our friendship. She had been telling me for months all the good things God was doing in her life. Her husband was really into church. My friend, in my

opinion, was a wild child. She was not a bad girl at all but she loved to have fun. I on the other hand was stiff and I was far from a wild child. Which is probably why we're friends, we had opposite personalities.
However, I knew that the man she married and the God she learned from him, changed her for the better. I wanted what she had. I did not want her husband, but I wanted to know the God they loved. I wanted my husband to love me the way her husband loved her. However, it did not work out that way. The Friday we arrived in ATL, my friend and I went out to eat. We enjoyed each other's company and I had shared with her marital issues and problems that were going on. On the way back to the hotel I remember her saying, "Let's pray." She prayed so hard that she began to speak in tongues or her prayer language. For a little Kentucky Catholic girl, this was a bit much. After she prayed she said, "Now you pray." I remember beginning my prayer the best way I knew how. I reminded God that He had allowed me to write some beautiful things but I could not come up with any words that suited my situation except 'Lord keep Satan away from my family' I prayed that over and over and over again until I was yelling and crying uncontrollably. In moments, I heard a weird little squeak or squeal, and I began to speak in tongues. It was real. I could not stop it. I lost control. The controlling spirit in me that always knew exactly what to do, was out of control. I continued to cry, babble, and moan. My friend followed the Spirit of God. She allowed me to cry for hours before she took me back

to the hotel. By this time I was still crying, huffing, and attempted to talk. I saw my grandmother first and said, "I don't know what just happened to me." After I attempted to tell the story in detail between my cries and huffs, Grandma said, "Child you just got saved and filled with the Holy Ghost." The small statement seemed to make me go right back to the crying, huffing, and moaning. However, I was not sad. I was not upset. And although I did not fully understand what happened, I knew I had experienced God in such a way that would impact my life forever. My grandmother continued to minister to me and pray. After several hours, my friend asked me to go to church with her the next morning. Even though the purpose of the trip was our new business, I realized God had different business He wanted me to learn, my Father's business. The feeling I felt the night right after my salvation can only be explained as terror because there was a war going on for me. God had won me to Him, but Satan was still trying to keep me in fear with him. My friend and her husband, who later guided me through my new experiences, allowed me to sleep on their coach. I remember distinctly drifting off to sleep and snapping out of the sleep because I felt like something or someone was watching me. I woke up in the middle of the night and saw a picture of Jesus on their mantle, and even that scared me. I can only explain the leading of the Holy Spirit that led me to get up off the couch and go to the bedroom of their two children. They had a third toddler bed that their son would sleep on when he visited. Whatever terror I felt, the Spirit of the Lord gave me peace knowing nothing would harm the children. So nothing would harm me. I curled up in that bed and slept. The interrupted sleep patterned continued through the night. At one point I woke up and stared out the window, and I saw what looked like a being in a hooded black robe. I curled up even tighter in the toddler bed afraid to move. This persisted all night. It had to be around 3 or 4 o'clock in the morning that a light so great in the room woke me. It was so bright I thought the sun had rose. I opened my eyes and the night was still there, but the hooded being was gone. After I went to sleep this final time, it was peaceful. I did not wake again until daybreak. I believe God allowed the light of angels to illuminate the room. And although I thought the sun had rose, it was the Son of God that rose in my life that night. The peace of God filled my soul. My friends got ready for church and loaded their two children in car seats. I humbly sat in the back seat with the children just as I had humbly laid on the toddler bed the prior evening. The Sunday school lesson title that morning was, ' Here I am Lord, send me', The text was Isaiah 6:1-8 it read, " In the year that King Uzziah died, I saw the Lord, high and exalted, seated on a throne; and the train of his robe filled the temple. 2 Above him were seraphim, each with six wings: With two wings they covered their faces, with two they covered their feet, and with two they were flying. 3 And they were calling to one another: 'Holy, holy, holy is the Lord Almighty; the whole earth is full of his glory.' 4 At the sound of their voices the doorposts and thresholds shook and the temple was filled with smoke.5 "Woe to me!" I cried. "I am ruined! For I am a man of unclean lips, and I live among a people of unclean lips, and my eyes have seen the King, the Lord Almighty."6 Then one of the seraphim flew to me with a live coal in his hand, which he had taken with tongs from the altar. 7 With it he touched my mouth and said, "See, this has touched your lips; your guilt is taken away and your sin atoned for. 8 Then I heard the voice of the Lord, saying, "Whom will I send? Who will go for us?" I said, "Here I am. Send me!" This text blessed my life in every direction. It helped me to come to grips with my past. I could not see God until my King Uzziah died, my soon to be ex-husband. Although I loved him, I allowed that love to be greater than my love for God. The text helped my present because I was one cussing little sister that was far from God. Yet once the presence of God entered that room, I slept humbly on a toddler bed, I found myself humbled, unfinished and in the presence of God. There would have been a time when the lack of control in this situation would have troubled me. However, I was at peace. And last but not least, I saw my future. Sunday morning in church school revealed who I wanted to become, a servant of God and for God. I wanted to be sent by God to do His work. I wanted to be a commercial for God! I left Georgia desiring to be used by God. The Lord led me to a church when I got back home in Kentucky that helped cultivate what God was doing in me. Up until that point, I had never sung in church. Yet now I was singing in church and pouring out my whole heart in one song, LORD MAKE ME A VESSEL. I wanted to be a vessel for God. I wanted to be a commercial for God. I wanted people to see God when they saw me. I can honestly say God did it. He caused me to be a commercial for born again Christians, recently divorced with children. Today I can say I understand what I wanted. However, back then I did not fully understand what I was asking God to do. The sentiment of the song expressed exactly what I wanted, LORD MAKE ME A VESSEL. So I became one of God's commercials for being saved, single, and parenting. However, being a commercial for God means, you want God to use you how He sees fit. So the honest truth is we do not get to dictate how God uses us. So then when He begins to use us in a mighty way we complain because His use of us is not quite what we anticipated. So with that being said, it took a while for me to comprehend my prayers had been answered. God was getting the glory out of the circumstances of my life. The problem was I hated my circumstances. I hated being single. I hated not being married. I hated being a single parent. I hated the divine detours of my life. But, I knew my change was real and my heart, mind, and soul was still in the same place, here I am Lord send me!

Lessons Learned
Chapter 4

Consider it pure joy, my brothers, when you are involved in various trials, because you know that the testing of your faith produces endurance. But you must let endurance have its full effect, so that you may be mature and complete, lacking nothing. James 1:2-4

As I previously shared, it took a while for me to accept that God's plan and my plan were not the same. I was learning all these new things in God that were truly exciting. And I remember specifically a Woman of God preaching and encouraging other women and men to write down what you wanted and what you wanted in a mate. So then I began to create different lists of thing I wanted from God. I had a list on steroids because it kept getting bigger and bigger. I wanted God to get me re-married so my children would have a daddy, I wanted God to get the home I wanted for my children, I wanted God to get my ministry rolling, and my money together. I had a list for my list and I wanted what I wanted. I wanted what I felt was best for me. God however wanted me to have a deeper understanding of Him and to use me in the midst of my circumstance. This is what I asked Him to do. God wanted to develop me. God wanted to teach me how to have joy in Him despite whatever circumstance I found myself. God desired to produce endurance in me so I could mature, be complete, and lack nothing. So after the salvation process had begun, my old life ended and my new life in Christ began. God desires to develop all of us. According to the Word of God, He desires to produce endurance in each of us. However, in order for endurance to be produced there must be something to endure. For me, it was my circumstances of being suddenly saved, single, and parenting. I was divorced, newly converted to Christianity, etc. etc. etc. We all are different and we all have different circumstances. However, God desires to help us work through the issues to show us how we are growing stronger in Him. What better way to show growth except through a test. Anytime we learn something new a test is sure to follow. The testing could be anything that tests your strength. However, the goal behind the testing is to grow you in mind, body, and spirit. The Bible says, in James 1:2-4 that we should consider it pure joy. The question is what is it that we are to consider as pure joy? The answer is trails. It is the trails of life that make us strong in God. However, the world likes to make folk believe that if you are in God everything and everyone will be perfect, and this is not true. We can never buy into what the world sells about our mighty God. What God teaches through the Word of God whether life is all right or all wrong, He is there! He will lead if we follow. He will never leave or forsake us. The purpose of the testing is to produce! God wants us to produce the endurance necessary to overcome the next big thing. Life is full of the next big problem, the next big issue, the next big thing that we need to overcome. So for my personal life, the testing came in the form of learning to accept the single parent role and allowing God to teach me what He wanted me to know. There were five basic lessons that have blessed my life beyond measure.

Lesson #1 BE CONSISTENT! The very first lesson God brought to me was be consistent in how I lived before my children. In other words, God does not want us to be a tongue talking, sanctified singing, Holy Ghost praying people of God at church. However, at home living fowl. So when I was at home my children saw me praying, speaking in tongues, singing and praising our Lord and Savior. These actions lined up with my life at church and home. He didn't want them to have bi-polar home situation that was nurtured in confusion. God is not a God of confusion, so then Church mama or daddy has to match at home mama or daddy. Be Consistent!

Lesson #2 Your Children are your LOVE CONNECTION. My list of things that I wanted included the man of my dreams. I wanted a new love connection because my first choice had failed. I wanted my new love connection to be my new man and my children's new father. I spent countless hours praying for this man I knew God wanted me to have. However, what God taught me during this time was how to make a love connection with Him and my babies. He wanted me to put all my attention and energy in Him and them. My divorce left me vulnerable so a new man without understanding of God and self would lead to destruction. Therefore He taught me how to seek a deeper love for Him and my children through the Word of God. Seeking God's face will help us make deeper connections to Him. His Word will lead us to deeper understanding of what love is all about. These efforts to make a connection with God and family will bless our lives and others.

Lesson #3 Be Holy for I am Holy. The truth is, this lesson was somewhat of a struggle because I wanted to be young, free, grown and sexy. God wanted me to be Holy because He was Holy. He sets the tone for mankind to follow Him. Our lives function better when we decide to commitment to follow God because among many things, He is a teacher. The lessons we learn following holiness brings new beginnings. These new beginnings that God teaches about holiness do not line up with the world. Therefore God will lead you to holiness but there will be many that encourage you to follow after your flesh. They will even tell you be young and 'sow your oats'. Beloved stay the course and chase after God and be holy because He is holy. His holiness produces a beauty that surpasses all understanding. Be Holy because God is Holy.

Lesson 4# Mercy is forever. I am grateful to God that I was taught by my parents to value myself. But, I still use to beat up on myself so bad when I had moments where I slipped up with a young, cute guy. He would say that he was ok with my four kids, but I only talked to him at night. It took God to teach me the young man was only interested in what he was interested in. I would spend weeks holding out because I wanted to be Holy because God was Holy. However, the young man wanted to get what he wanted. So even if it took him 3 or 4 months to get me, he got me, until I got tire of that game. I would spiral into self-hate and shame. I would wonder why God would ever want to use me. However, God desired to teach me that the mercy of God was forever. It wasn't that God was trying to teach me to use His compassionate character as a free pass to do whatever I wanted. But God wanted to teach me that He is a compassionate God. A great example is one evening I started off proud of myself for lasting close to 18 months of celibacy. However, by the end of the evening, I crying in a puddle of tears because I had failed again. I cried so long until I felt the Spirit of God fill me with His peace. I asked God why he even dealt with me because I felt like I was always messing up. However, God took me to a Psalm that described the Mercy of God. He allowed me to immediately understand it was His compassion or mercy that was there. Again it was not to give me a free pass, but to understand that God is compassionate and He knew I was trying. This lesson I will never forget because it applies to everything. Mercy is forever.

Lesson 5# His Grace is sufficient. When you enter into the classroom of the Holy Spirit, He can use anything to teach you. We can experience our lives falling apart yet God will teach us that the grace

He gives is enough to get us through. Quality time takes effort, and effort can leave you exhausted. The homework after school. The after school programs. Overtime at work. Church programs and choir practice. The football, track, basketball, dance and whatever else team that demands time will leave you exhausted. However, God's unmerited favor helps you find balance. Being saved, single, and parenting will bring a gamut of feelings that may bring a tidal wave of overwhelming emotion. However, God is the Jehovah Shamah that means He is there. His grace will help us manage the lives of our children as well as ourselves because the old Christian saying is He will not place more on you than you can bear. Therefore, His grace is sufficient

Four Models of Single Parents
Chapter 5

And if it seem evil unto you to serve the LORD, choose you this day whom ye will serve; whether the gods which your fathers served that were on the other side of the flood, or the gods of the Amorites, in whose land ye dwell: but as for me and my house, we will serve the LORD.
Joshua 24:15

The goal in these next few pages is not to make you feel bad if you see a reflection of yourself. However, if you do see a reflection of yourself and you don't like it, remember that is why we need and love Jesus. He can fix it and us!

1) The Foolish Woman

Proverbs 14:1 A wise woman builds her house, but the foolish plucks it down with her hands. I read in the Sermon Commentary Bible, "If you ask what God and the word of God mean by wisdom and folly, the answer will embrace three particulars: on the side of wisdom, these—forethought, earnestness, perseverance; on the side of folly, in like manner, these— improvidence, irresolution, unsteadiness. Corresponding to these three qualities of the builder are the three conditions of building: (1) To build you must have a plan; (2) building requires toil. (3) The proof of the building is growth..." A foolish woman does not exhibit forethought and does not have a plan that she has committed to the Lord. Therefore, without a plan she plans to fail by default. As a single parent it is our job to expose our children to things outside of our personal communities. This requires work and research of ways to plan or seek out ways to bring new experiences to our children. Some single moms have more money than others. However, the lack of means should not stop any parent. We must persevere! When I was raising my children without financial help from their dad at the time, I would save money each year for a zoo pass. Two or three times a week we would enter the Louisville Zoo. We would learn about the different animals and have a picnic. Somedays we would even go to Joe Cresson Park across the street and play. My point this didn't require a lot of money but it did require me to plan my finances out so I could buy the yearly zoo pass. I would have to plan meals that were fun for children picnicking in the zoo or park. And just because my money was funny and my change was strange, I still could persevere with a plan to expose my children to something different and new. A foolish woman does not have a plan to build her children up and so then she tears them down because she lacks the desire to work. We have to work at building a steady and balanced home. A balanced home provides intellectual and spiritual outlets to help each child grow. Church is another way to expose our children to choices that teach how to build up verses pluck down. Having a plan will not make things perfect, however it will give us a goal to reach for. And when we have a sincere interest in our children, we can in turn earnestly seek God's face to help build a balanced home. A foolish Woman that keeps God out of the equation truly parents alone. She forfeits the help that God gives to build her home. Therefore, without the help of God the home is not steady, it fails to provide spiritual guidance, therefore it falls short of creating a safe haven for the children to flourish.

2) The Missing Man

Luke 14:28-30 For which of you, desiring to build a tower, does not first sit down and count the cost, whether he has enough to complete it? Otherwise, when he has laid a foundation and is not able to finish, all who see it begin to mock him, saying, 'This man began to build and was not able to finish.' If a foolish woman tears her house down, than a missing father failed to count the cost. In both cases, the woman and the man are missing the importance of family. There are many that may push the thought process, 'a man is not necessary in the family'. However God's thought process is quite the opposite. God created man and woman because they contribute differently to the family. There are many things I could say about a father. However, when the words are reduced to their lowest denominator, a father is there! Whatever happens in our lives, a father that has made the decision to support his family is there physically, emotionally, and financially. A missing father, however, has not counted the cost of starting a family. A missing father has missed the mission. He is unable to contribute to the family unit because he chooses not to be there. Therefore the dynamics of the home can be out of balance, missing male influence, experiencing immature emotional and spiritual growth, and the list goes on because the father parent is needed. Often people pick out the physically missing fathers. They do not contribute and it's a mess. We get it. A father is needed. However, we fail to discuss the fathers that are in the home but are not there. Matt. 6:33, says, "Seek ye first the kingdom of God and His righteousness and all these things shall be added..." There are fathers that are in the home but chasing after money, cars, houses, drugs, alcohol, etc. They are physically in the home but there is an emotional and spiritual disconnect. You dear sir, you are still missing in action. You may be physically sleeping in the home but failing to contribute emotionally, spiritually, and sometimes financially. Therefore they are like phantom fathers, you can't see their influence. This further hinders the family from progressing into a healthy family.

3) The Double-Minded Parent

James 1:8 being a double- minded man, unstable in all his ways. As I stated previously, my first lesson God taught me was to be consistent with my children. He did not want me to confuse my children with my actions. The only reason a parent lives one way at church and another life at home is they are unstable. The problem with an unstable parenting is you don't know what you will get. The bi-polar tendencies disrupt the home and create an emotional roller coaster. When we think of instability, our thoughts gravitate to things that cannot support. A financial venture with unstable revenue flow has problems. A leader without a plan is an unstable person to follow, and a house without a foundation will not stand. There are many forms of instability that simply do not support. A double minded parent has ways that cannot be trusted. The home has unclear expectations because the parent continues to shift what is important. Take for instance, the parent feels this week, 'church is the answer!' so much time that week is spent on church activity, studies, and gatherings. However, the very next week this same parent feels church is inconvenient, boring, and time consuming. The instability may not be physically spoken to the children but actions speak louder than words. If we decide that our home will be a home where God flows, we must choose to serve Him. Joshua 24:15 says, "But if serving the LORD seems undesirable to you, then choose for yourselves this day whom you will serve, whether the gods your ancestors served beyond the Euphrates, or the gods of the Amorites, in whose land you are living...." Instead of serving God, there are some parents that serve the many little gods of our time that compete for our interest when really there should be no competition. However, they seek to worship the little gods of musical icons, super athletes, and movie stars. If they like it, we like it. If they go, we go. If they say it's ok, then it must be because we serve them instead of the God that saves, heals, redeems, and changes lives. A double minded parent conveys unstable thinking to the dynamics of the home and the children are confused as to what is important and what is rubbish?

4) The Saved Single Parent

Let us first understand that a saved single parent is not perfect. However, the saved single parent has made a choice to lead the family to and live for God. Joshua 24:15 goes on to say "...But as for me and my household, we will serve the LORD." The leader of the home decided everyone in my house will serve the Lord. The choice was made to put God at the head of the family even it cost you face with family and friends. Let me use myself as an example. I remember when I first got saved. I was serious and I made a choice for my home not to indulge Halloween. Many of my family members did not like my choice, including my own mother, God rest her soul. She was a woman of God, minister of the Gospel and lover of the Word, but she felt Halloween was fun and a tradition that my children should not be denied. I truly did respect her opinion, but it was not her choice. Mother did not live in my home therefore, I had to do what worked for me based on where God was taking me and my family. My house was going to serve the Lord and I choose NO HALLOWEEN. When October 31st rolled around, I would treat them to the movies, bowling, sometimes both. However, the only name I wanted my children to hallow was the Lord Jesus Christ. Again, as for me and my house, we will serve the Lord. There will come many times in our lives as saved single parents when we have to make a decision for our home that works for us but others will not understand it. Sometimes family, friends and the world will push you to make decisions that they are comfortable with but that is not what God told you to do! People will try to control the way you see something without offering you the freedom of choice. At least God gives us the opportunity to choose! For the Word says, "Choose ye this day who you going to serve..." Making choices to serve Jesus means, we make choices for our families and their well-being. There will always be people that challenge our faith, choices, and walk with God. Remember making a choice to do it God's way will always be the best choice. But it will not always be an easy choice because it typically conflicts with others and the way they think you should handle any given situation. However, if you truly desire to be a Successful Saved Single parent then you must boldly choose the ONE God, follow Him and be done.

The Dynamics of Influence- Chapter 6

What shall we then say to these things? If God be for us, who can be against us? Nay, in all these things we are more than conquerors through him that loved us. Romans 8:31, 37 (KJV)

As a saved, single and parenting parent, we cannot afford to fail in the dynamics of influence. Dynamics is defined as a pattern or process of change, growth, or activity. And influence is defined as the power to change or affect someone or something. So then it is our job as parents to pay attention to people that have an affect over our children that leads to unwanted patterns. If we are alert, we can determine if the dynamics of the relationship is good or bad for our children. The Bible speaks of different types of influences that are important as we raise our children. 1 Corinthians 15:33 says, "...Do not be deceived: bad company corrupts good moral." I cannot express it enough as parents, we have to be alert to the company our children keep. We have to notice when we see a change in their demeanor and decision making process. Typically this could be based on the influences of others that may expose our children to things that are not healthy and ultimately change them for the worse. Bad company does not always expose children to drugs, alcohol, and sex, but bad company may expose your child to a way of thinking that challenges what you are teaching or sometimes your very relationship. I remember several years back my eldest daughter had two friends whose company she enjoyed. However, both these young girls did not have the influence of their mothers. Therefore everything I expressed to my daughter as an expectation, they challenged and encouraged her to disobey me and follow them. Had I not been alert to what God was showing me, the relationships may have developed deeper while creating a wedge between my daughter and me. The minute God allowed me to understand this bad company was corrupting my daughter, I brought it to her attention. I never told her she could not keep company with these two young girls. However, I did explain to her their experiences and perspectives with their moms were totally different than her relationship with me. At first my daughter felt I was just being over protective. However because I also had influence over my daughter she was able to listen and be alert. She was able to see for herself what I was talking about. They had subtle, little, ugly things to say about me or the way I instructed her. They had totally teen age comments that fit their age. However, since I still had some influence in her life, she did not jump on the "MEAN MAMA" band wagon. She listened, paid attention, and made a more informed decision. She was able to stand firm on what she knew and not cave in due to the pressure of her peers. This does not mean there were not moments when she elected to make those same normal teen age goofy decisions, but God helped me to have an observant eye. I then in turn taught her how to be observant and avoid some potentially dangerous situations. So even though it appears to be the age old over-protective mommy demeanor, the results are still the same. Pay attention to the friends and even family that create a circle of influence in your child's life.

The Circle of Influence

When I was raising my children, I had a very small circle of people that I trusted. Many family members and even some friends felt I was over protective of my children. I suppose there was some truth in their observations, but I was under the firm belief that God and I were all my children had. The Bible states in James 1:5 "If any of you lacks wisdom, he should ask God, who gives generously to all without finding fault, and it will be given to him..." So I spent a lot of time asking God for the wisdom to follow Him as I raised my children. So God showed me early on in my single parenting journey to use the wisdom He gave generously. Therefore, I paid close attention to who I dated. I paid even closer attention to who I introduced to my children. In 8 years of being single, my children only met two of my friends because I was serious about them. Although I introduced my children to my two friends I still schooled my children about inappropriate behavior. I always left the door open for them to speak to me openly about whatever was on their mind. I am not a child psychologist, psychiatrist, or family therapist. However, the wisdom of God and His anointing go a very long way! This is not meant to bash any of these professions. Their knowledge is needed and blessed when given with God at its core. However, God wanted to teach me how to lean on Him. He wanted me to understand the power of His wisdom and His might. Like any parent, I am biased about all my children. I believe they are all beautiful, handsome and built well. Therefore, I always had to keep my eye on them, and I told them regularly about their beauty so that they heard it from me first. Raising my daughters there was a frame of reference because I was once a young girl. However raising my son was different because I was never a boy and could never teach him how to be a man. I would often become insulted if people called him 'my little man' because he was not. He was my son. It is so easy for people to protect their daughters and not allow them to go with people that they may feel have questionable motives. However, for a son sometimes people possess a similar less protective thought, 'oh let him be a boy.' So when different men from the church, family or friends wanted to take him on outings, I had to trust God to show me those men and their motive. Now some folk think just because a sister or brother is in the church everything is kosher. However, the wisdom of God will teach you that the church is a hospital and it takes God's grace, mercy and a litany of other things to help us overcome our past, obstacles, trials, and tribulations. With that being said, I didn't trust people easily with my daughter's or my son. There was a man across the street from us and he was married with a child, but he didn't have any sons. I never allowed my kids to go into the houses of others so that when I looked outside for them, I could see them easily. However, I noticed my son going over to this man's house quite a bit. My son would hang out on his bike and talk to this gentleman. After a few visits, I asked my son, "What are you talking to him about?" My son's response was "all kinds of stuff." My son informed me that this gentleman had helped him fix the chain on his bike and they talked about cars. I believed him because this man was always under the hood of a car or fixing things around his home. God allowed me to be at peace with this man and he continued to pour into my son his love of cars and fixing them. One afternoon, I was able to greet my neighbor. I advised him in kindness that if my son ever got on his nerves just send him home. The gentleman proceeded to inform me he was not any trouble and loved having him around. He went on to say that he was raised by a single mother and he understood the drama I faced as a single parent. God allowed this relatively quiet man to show my son things that a man typically shows a boy. God allowed my son to learn about something that he loved and loves even to this day, cars and fixing things. God also showed me there will be people I can trust and some I cannot trust. One year there was a young musician in the church that persistently asked if my daughter could go with him and some friends after church. At first she really wanted to go and hang out with him. So God gave me wisdom to let her go along with all her siblings, and dinner was on him. I would tell my son, and daughter not to leave her with him alone. It worked for me. After several conversations later, my daughter lost interest in his invitations. We both found out later, he liked young girls. In the end, it was not a great surprise because God knew it and unlike my neighbor across the street, I was uneasy about the invitations. He showed me how to keep my integrity as a Christian and a parent but give them freedom to grow, learn, and make healthy decisions. The lesson God showed me in both of these circumstances is there will always be people that mean well and imposters that try to enter into the circle of influence, but the wisdom of God help you discern if the person means well or alert you there is a breach.

When the Circle of Influence is Broken

Single parenting is not a series of crossed "t's and dotted "I's" there will be successful moments and then there will be moments of failure. However, as earlier discussed there is favor in the failure if you allow God to teach you through each experience. God does not want us to focus on the many mistakes that we will make while being a single parent. He wants us to trust Him and receive the grace that God gives to continue to raise our children. Another way to understand the favor of God is gaining God's approval or acceptance even in the failure. God desires for us to learn from our failures and continue! The Bible puts it like this in Romans 8:31, 37, "What then, shall we say in response to these things? If God is for us, who can be against us?" and then verse 37, "No, in all these things we are more than conquerors through him who loved us...." Life will always present situations where our circle of influence is broken. During these times, we may experience moments of mistrust for our children or the people that have broken the circle of influence. And because we are human, we may not take the Jesus road. We may fall to the flesh but, we must understand that God always has our back and is in our corner. That does not mean that God will always like our approach or response to some situations. Therefore there may be times when God has to redirect our emotions, motive, and spiritual understanding. However through it all, God wants us to know that He is for us even if the world is against us! So then our love for God opens us up to greater wisdom and understanding when we accept God and how He does things. God will teach us that we are overcomers and more than conquerors through Jesus Christ. He will show us through His Word how to break free from the prison of unforgiveness and move forward in the freedom of forgiveness.

The Freedom of Forgiveness versus the Imprisonment of Unforgiveness

Chapter 7

Now the Lord is that Spirit: and where the Spirit of the Lord is, there is liberty.
2 Corinthians 3:17

I remember several years back looking at an episode of The Fresh Prince of Belair. This story-line was about Will's dad coming back in his life only to leave him again. The last scene was Will falling into Uncle Phil's arms and whimpering, "Why does he not want me?" I remember bursting into tears because this was the first time God allowed me to understand that my choices had caused pain for my children. The pain they may have been feeling was sometimes seen and there were moments when the pain was not seen. I even wrote a song about the emotion I felt from that night. The simple sitcom episode took me into the classroom of the Holy Spirit. It triggered me to thinking and remembering that the choices that I make and made for my life affected my children. I grew in my relationship with God to understand the concept of forgiveness but there were moments when I made the choice to go headlong in unforgiveness and grudge holding. I was resentful that he got to move on with his life and I was left behind raising our children on my own. I resented the fact that the love we had had failed us all so miserably. I resented single parenting because it did not fit what I wanted for my children. Just like the character from "Fresh Prince of Belair", I felt like why does he not want me and why does he not want our children? The pain of this resentfulness began to imprison me in unforgiveness. This can be a very subtle process that causes you to become a bitter person. And the truth was, I was becoming a bitter and unforgiving person. Look at the definition of unforgiving which means unwilling to forgive but when I dug a little deeper into the definition I found unforgiving meant very harsh, difficult: not allowing weakness or error. The unforgiving atmosphere I had created for myself did not allow my ex-husband to mess up nor did it allow me to get over the mess up and get on with my life. It took time for me to recognize that I had to forgive him. Whatever the reason was, I had to accept it and move on so I could get to living. Before I came to this understanding, I would spend hours thinking of things I could have done, should have done or would have done. I would agonize over things that he did that hurt me to my core that made it difficult to move. So then I became a voluntary paraplegic. I was paralyzed in a past love that was long gone and imprisoned in a dream that was now detoured to a different journey. I had to make the choice to get on the new journey God was providing or stay stuck. The song that I wrote starts out like this,"...seems like my choices caused seen and unseen pain..." Our choices to move or to stay affect our children in many different ways. I thank God I was not in a physically abusive marriage, but I know some people who were and they chose to stay. The choice caused unseen pain in their children that surfaced in different ways from stealing, fighting and, abusive behaviors. The list goes on but the issue is the same, choose better, choose wiser, and become stronger so you can break free from the imprisonment of unforgiveness! I have this saying I say all the time. 'I know what it is like to be a slave and I know what it is like to be free and I love freedom so much better.' So when I experienced the liberty of God, it was refreshing. The Spirit of God allows us to find liberty in Him. So then that liberty encourages us to walk in the empowerment that God brings when we choose Him. My new found freedom or liberty allowed me to learn I could do bad all by myself and I didn't need him. I needed Jesus. I learned how to explore who I wanted to become and move past who I used to be. So then I began to believe the Scripture, Philippians 4:13 " I can do all things through Christ who strengthens me". I found myself going back to school and getting my degree. I was smiling more. I re- married. I became an author and business woman. I preached better. I taught better. Stevie Wonder penned the song, "There is something about your love" He may have been talking about a woman but it was something about the love of Jesus Christ that knocked me off my feet. However I landed on my knees which helped me develop a prayer life.

Developing a Prayer life
Chapter 8

Continue in prayer, and watch in the same with thanksgiving; Colossians 4:2 (KJV)

I grew up among praying women and men. I had grandmothers, grandfather, mother, father, uncles and aunts who all knew the power of prayer. I remember specifically my mother in her later years spending hours praying in her office/prayer room. She would bombard heaven as a righteous woman with prayers, laments, supplication, and prayers of praise to our most high God. I learned from her how to continually seek God's face for help. I love the word develop because in your mind's eye you can see parts of things that are coming together or being developed. This is a clear description of my prayer life of my past, present, and future. We will always have a developing prayer life if we remain in the Lord. There is a song that my grandmother use to sing. It starts out, "...Somebody prayed for me they had me on their mind they took a little time and prayed for me. I'm so glad they prayed, I'm so glad they prayed, I'm so glad they prayed for me..." This song always creates a Holy Ghost tidal wave of reflection and emotion because God has been faithful to have someone praying for me and my children. However, as my walk with God improved I learned that Jesus got up early in the morning to pray. So when I saw this in the Word of God, it became my heart's desire to have Morning Prayer and the Lord helped me to develop prayer time. Later on a visiting minister came to the church where I attended at the time and God allowed him to testify about how he and his family had morning devotion. Along with other ministers that God placed in my path that had family morning prayer and devotion. So then I started getting my children up for prayer and devotion. They did not like morning devotion, in fact, they hated it. However I am the parent, so they did it. As time passed and they got older they began to appreciate their time with God and understanding the blessing of an answered prayer. There were some mornings that I did not wake them but God led me to go and pray over each child and prophesy over their lives. As a mother that spent time with her children, God showed me their strengths and weaknesses. So He would lead me to speak God's plans over their lives and to stand firm on His Word that God's plan was to help them, help others, and help the Kingdom of God but not hurt them. As adults today, my children and I laugh at our morning devotions. Not because they were bad, but they were consistent. They knew we were going to get up for prayer almost every morning. This practice is something they continue in their personal lives today. I thank God for giving me the wisdom to pray over my children, pray over the husband that would eventually come, (Bless you Sr. Pastor Dominic Hunter), pray over the jobs they would one day receive, the spouses that would love them the way God loves them. It was and is that consistent prayer life that has helped my family. So I can't leave this conversation without encouraging you to pray for your children and to teach them how and when to pray. There is a simple acronym that I used personally and to teach them.

    1) PRAISE God before you ask God for anything.

    2) REPENT before God the things you have done wrong.

    3) ACCEPT the will of God

    4) YIELD to Him the people, situations, and circumstances that concern you.

Prayer is a conversation with God that can change things but typically it changes you. There will be many nights that you pray for your family. However, you may not see the immediate results of this prayer because God knows when we are ready to change. Although I spent countless hours praying to God, for a husband, I was not ready to change. When God blesses you with a wife or a husband, you have to surrender to God so you can turn over authority that belongs to the mate. And since I had spent years being both parents, God had to get me ready for a husband. Learning to surrender to the wife that will nurture the home that may be distinctly different from your no nonsense approach. The point is whether you are waiting for a husband or wife, you will have to change your single parent point of view, and that takes prayer. God seeks to teach us how to develop a prayer life that will bless our lives and the lives of our family, friends, and even strangers beyond measure. However, He knows when we are ready to take ownership of the necessary changes those prayers will bring. I am so grateful that God did not give me men when I thought I was ready. I am grateful that there were prayers He did not answer because they did not fit the will of God for my life. We have to accept the will of God for each season of our lives. God grants favor to receive our season of singleness if we accept His direction. Don't waste valuable time whining through your prayer about whatever. Accept that God has not forgotten you or your family. So keep praising, raising and praying for your children and others. The suddenness of singleness, salvation, and single parenting can be overwhelming. However the love, patience, and power of God will push you to keep praying in the trenches for your children, others, and yourself. Although you will encounter moments where you want to throw in the towel, know that God is there to lead and direct you to your right destiny. He is faithful to keep you on the mind of someone that is praying for you. A consistent prayer life will not only help you but God may allow you to see the results of a manifested prayer life. All that means is God may allow you see your prayers answered in His time and season. However, no matter what happens remain faithful and keep on praying.

Each Path is Different
Chapter 9

For I know the thoughts that I think toward you, saith the LORD, thoughts of peace, and not of evil, to give you an expected end.
Jeremiah 29:11 (KJV)

    We have looked at a lot of information about being suddenly saved, single, and single parenting. However, it is so important to point out that each person's path is different. A great example are those huge, beautiful homes. They are all brick with big porches and even bigger pools. The trees cover the land and the grass seems so green. As you drive by, you may wonder how did they get there? The path the person took to get that super huge home with all the trimmings was different. Some were doctors, lawyers, politicians the list goes on. The point is there were different ways to get there. It stands to reason that the people that typically occupy these homes had to go through something. Therefore we can never forget that every path we encounter in our lives requires faith in God to get there. This book is to encourage each reader to accept their situation of single parenting and expect God to meet you there. He promises that He will never leave you or forsake you. So then just because other people dropped you, does not mean God will not drop you! He has already purposed in His heart to help us and not to harm us. However just because God has a plan to give us a hope and a future, (Jer 29:11) does not mean we do nothing. We have to be willing to walk the path we have been given and stand boldly knowing God is there! We have to be willing to put in the work it takes to finish. Single parenting takes faith and work. They cannot exist without the other. The Bible says in James 2:20-22 Intl Standard Version "James 2:20 Do you want proof, you foolish person, that faith without actions is worthless? James 2:21 Our ancestor Abraham was justified by his actions when he offered his son Isaac on the altar, wasn't he? James 2:22 you see that his faith worked together with what he did, and by his actions his faith was made complete." God intends to help our faith be complete. Our faith has to work together with our actions. Therefore just like Abraham did something, we have to do something. We have to put what we have learned into action. God desires to help you every step of the way. Do not waste a lot of unnecessary time mumbling and grumbling about your unwanted circumstances. As I develop and continue to develop into a better Christian, God has allowed me to understand my circumstances better. My path of single parenting had very little influence from my children's father. However no matter how the father of my children failed, it was my job to teach them Christian values. This was my path. God knew there would come a day when he wanted to be a part of their lives again. So I had to teach them Christian principles that unwrapped the gift of forgiveness for them and myself. It is forgiveness that allows my grown children to this day to move forward with their relationship with their father. This progress however came because as a parent I chose Jesus for my household and I insisted that they learn God's way of doing things. Therefore, God showed me a better path that did not involve bad- mouthing their dad. God helped me to understand forgiveness and move forward. God showed me how to avoid allowing the past to hold me hostage which in turn would hold them hostage. And for everything that I learned, I tried to pass the knowledge on to our children. As time has gone by, they are now adults. However, they do not hate their father. God gives us all room to fall, fail, overcome, and even conquer our circumstance because we choose to journey with Jesus. I cannot stress enough each path of single parenting will be different and similar but it is uniquely ours to embrace, learn from it and allow God to show you the path for you and your children. He knows how to grow us through our circumstances and help us embrace our personalized path.

Suddenly Saved and Single- It is important to understand life falls in FIRST THINGS FIRST categories. What I mean by this is when we master the concept of focusing on the things that come first we will realize that other things will fall into place. The salvation process is the first thing that makes all of life make sense and it causes things to fall into place. The second thing that has to happen is we must accept our single parenting status. When we walk in and own our single parent status, we can make better choices for our children. I am so saddened when I hear about, read about, look on the news and see single parents that put their lust relationship first instead of their children's well- being. I use lust relationships because a love relationship sent by God will not put you in a situation where you choose your lover over the lover of your soul and the children that God allowed you to bear. However, Christian society has accepted that this behavior is acceptable because we do not lovingly confront the behavior. Love is the only way to help someone see they have missed the mark. Every time we do not take the opportunity to tell that single parent in our circle of influence that the woman or man that they are so in love should not be greater than the love they show God. His love is all encompassing and perfected to cover everything and everyone who wants it. We are accepting this foolish behavior and we inadvertently tell the persons it is ok to live life out of order. So then we have to take time to teach parents how to show and sow. This means we show our children during their youth years that they are loved and special and then we sow into them our time, love, and talents to solidify and confirm they are wanted. Then when God does send our mate the fruits of the love you have sown into God and His children will be evident. We have opportunities to take as parents single or two parent homes to sow into the lives of our children. We make choices to sow love, hope, peace, joy, security, and the list goes on because the efforts of parenting never ends. Even when they are adults they will always be your child.

You know they have developed into grown men and women but they will always be your baby. So the instinct to take care of them should never goes away. However, among us are single parents that failed to show and sow into the lives or their children. The disheartening results can leave us overwhelmed. There was a song in the 70's called, THE CATS IN THE CRADLE. It was sung by Harry Chapin. The song opens with a child arriving in the world. The child learned to walk, talk, and grew but the daddy was catching planes and paying bills. So the child makes the observation and affirmation that he wants to be just like his daddy. The hook of the song is the question asked by the child, "when you coming home, dad?" And the response by the dad is "I don't know when, but we'll get together then son. You know we will have a good time then..." The song is about reaping and sowing the father delays the right to sow time into the life of his son, and the son has already affirmed he wants to be just like his father continuing the negligence. Therefore the end of the song is the same as the beginning, only this time it is the father that wants the time and attention from his grown son. The father is attempting to reap where he has not sown. Therefore, there was no harvest. We live in a time where we have many single parents and two parent homes that attempt to reap from the lives of their children where they have not sown time, love, hope or anything of value. The father in the song valued chasing after money over spending time with his child. The father valued chasing after planes and paying the next bill over having a moment to listen to his child. The point that is important not to miss is that things have value but they are not as valuable as the opportunity to develop a lasting relationship with your child. Some single parents attempt to overcompensate their children with things instead of quality time. Therefore the child grows up with a mis-managed value system that is not beneficial towards their adult life. Money is helpful but it does not replace you. I spent a lot of time thinking that if I had more money I would be able to do more for my children. The things I thought they needed were just to occupy them because, the truth was they needed me. So whatever we did whether it required a lot of money or a dollar or two, my kids wanted me and I wanted them. It took a while but I finally received what God had been saying to me, trust in Him and He will direct my path. Allowing God to direct my path eliminated the need to chase after money. Therefore, I made better choices to show them I loved them by sowing into their lives and allowing God to lead me in the right direction. As single parents we cannot reap from the lives of our children where we have not sown. If you remember the four models of a single parent, three of the models reflect levels of selfishness that do not edify the family. So when we allow God to re-direct our path He shows us how to show and sow love.

SEX

Chapter 10

Therefore if any man be in Christ, he is a new creature: old things are passed away; behold, all things are become new.
2 Corinthians 5:17

The topic of being suddenly saved, single, and parenting cannot end without discussing SEX! The approach to the topic of sex in the Christian arena is simple yet complex. The simplicity of the topic is what does God say? One of my favorite scriptures that helped me repeatedly when I was single was 1 Corinthians 6:18-20. "Flee from sexual immorality. Every other sin a person commits is outside the body, but the sexually immoral person sins against his own body. Or do you not know that your body is a temple of the Holy Spirit within you, whom you have from God? You are not your own for you were bought with a price. So glorify God in your body..." I believe the part of this text that I mastered was FLEE FROM SEXUAL IMMORALITY because that was the only action I felt I could take against fornication. If he looked at me too long, I would flee. If he asked for my name and his voice was deep, I would flee. If we engaged in meaningful conversation, I would sprint away! The simplicity of what God expected was do not have sex outside of marriage. However, sometimes I could get lost in my emotion and that would almost always lead to sex. Therefore my greatest action against fornication was to flee to God. So for me, I would drown myself in ministry, music, work, raising my children. I did whatever I needed to do to keep me from jumping from one man's bed to the next. This was how God allowed me to keep my body as a temple for the Holy Spirit. Now remember each person has their own story of how they handled sex God's way during their singleness. This is how I did it, ministry. I can honestly say, I was no angel. However, I can equally honestly say, I strived to honor my father in heaven. It is another one of my heart's desires to deal with this topic with genuineness and honestly. It was hard. It was frustrating. It was lonely. Because as much as I knew about God, I still was human and I recognized what I wanted was what I wanted. Matthew 11:28-29 says, "Come unto me, all ye that labor and are heavy laden, and I will give you rest. Take my yoke upon you, and learn of me; for I am meek and lowly in heart: and ye shall find rest unto your souls…" So I took the scripture at face value and I went to Jesus and the labor of trying to keep myself from bed hoping became less difficult, less frustrating, and less lonely. As time passed, I got better at glorifying God through my body by remembering it was the temple of the Holy Spirit. However, I want to spend a little time on when I was not glorifying God with my body because it was during those times the enemy would get in my head and make me feel horrible. The line of guilt that worked best with me was failing God. I always felt like I failed

God each time my feelings, hormones, and emotions led me to the bedroom. However, instead of God taking the opportunity to make me feel worse, He comforted me. God in His infinite wisdom and knowledge had every right to deliver the strictest of punishment yet He showed me kindness. He taught me how to stay out of the situations that lead me outside of His will by avoiding late night calls from men. I stopped going in to talk or to watch a movie because this led to ungodly situations. God didn't give up on me nor did He allow me to give up on myself. God has a way of getting down in the trenches with you to help you up not place His foot on your head. Marvin Sapp's song says, I was stronger, wiser, and better. Just like a child learning to walk, there will be moments when you fall down. However God, like any good parent, loves His children. He helps and convicts them of the wrong without condemning them. The use of conviction is to help us avoid the situation again. However, anything that is condemned is deemed unrepairable. God wants us to know that with Him we can be repaired, restored, and most of all redeemed. So again in the most simple message about sex and being suddenly saved, single and parenting is God does not want us to have sex before marriage. However, He is merciful and a God of another chance. Strive hard and know that He is God and the only way to please Him is to approach Him with faith and a desire to continue to seek Him. If you do this, the Scriptures say you will please Him. (Hebrews 11:6)

You have Worth and You are Worth It

In order to teach our children that they have worth, we must first believe it for ourselves. We live in a society where some parents have not been taught they have worth. Therefore it is difficult to pass something on to your child that you never had. We must never forget the Word of God says that we are fearfully and wonderfully made. (Psalms 139:14) So we must know no matter how we look that we are beautiful and we have worth. It is equally important to understand that you are worth it. It is so easy to get caught up into buying the things that they need and want but depriving ourselves of the few creature comforts that make life fun. So don't forget you. One day your children will grow up and move on to the plan that God has for their lives. If you have invested all your time and efforts into your children and nothing for yourself, you may experience the results of abandoning yourself. It is easy to leave behind the dreams and aspirations we once had for our lives in an effort to help our children reach their dreams. Balance is key. With the help of God, He will show us how to balance the things for our children as well as ourselves. Don't forget to give yourself sometime to remember that you have worth and you are worth it. If we continue to remember to bless ourselves, we are teaching ourselves to love ourselves. Learning to love self comes in handy when you are single. You have to know your worth because there are so many people that desire to use you for their own purposes. I remember a young dude that I really didn't find attractive. As a matter of fact I did not find him even interesting. However, every woman knows when a man is giving her the eye. I can say I felt surprised at the time because I was in my 30's and he was in his middle 20's. I never let on that I felt he was attracted to me. Months went by and I overheard him talking to a co-worker about how he didn't mind an older woman or even a woman with kids, if she knew what was up. I think the conversation was meant for me to hear and as I listened further, I began to understand what he was saying. He meant that a single woman with children or even an older single woman with children was good enough for sex but that is it. So the vibe I was feeling was not an attraction to me at all. It was a lust to have his way with me and his purpose for me had the potential for that moment to erase my worth if I let him. If I didn't know my worth, whatever he offered I would have accepted. God spent time growing me up spiritually to understand Him so I could understand me. And if we understand and love ourselves, we learn our self- worth. And when we know what we have worth, we do not accept rubbish. The Bible refers to us as a new creation. (Corinthians 2 5:17) So since we are not simply re- generated but the new creation has come. Once we are in Christ the old has passed away and we are made new in Him. When we have Jesus in our lives, we develop a greater understanding of life, self, worth, and love. So never forget you have been made whole in Christ Jesus. The wholeness we learn through the Word of God helps us mend together the frayed pieces of our lives. Prior to Christ, our lives may have been fragmented and in broken pieces. However, once we accept Christ as our Savior He helps us to pick up the pieces. God shows us how to extract the power from the pain of the broken pieces. He shows us how to put our lives together again through Christ Jesus. As a new creation in Christ we learn to take baby steps accepting God's love so we can love ourselves and know that we have worth and are worth it!

It's Complicated
Chapter 11

Above all, my brothers and sisters, do not swear oaths by heaven or by earth or by anything else. Instead, let your "Yes" mean yes and your "No" mean no! Otherwise, you may fall under condemnation. James 5:12

All you need to say is a simple "yes" or "no." Otherwise you will be condemned." I typically hear this statement from single women or women that are about to become single. They often refer to the previous relationship or marriage as complicated. I remember this phase of my singleness. I was headed to divorce court but I still very much loved my husband. The truth is he had moved on with his new boo and baby. However, the love I had was real and could be triggered by a text, a call, even the smell of his old cologne. Another honest confession is it took God to reveal to me that these TRIGGERS, if left to their own devices, could catapult me into confusion. 1 Corinthians 14:33 reads, "...For God is not the author of confusion, but of peace..." The triggers messed with my peace and therefore I could get caught up in the author of the triggers which was the Devil. So God's supernatural spiritual strength helped me to stay out of complicated situations.

Let's look at a few complicated situations:

Still Allowing Him or Her to Contribute to Life Situations

Still allowing him or her to contribute to life situations other than for the children. This is complicated because this person has given up rights to have a say in what you do with your life. The children should always come first and will demand conversation. However, trust God to show you how to move on from the emotional connections that you once shared with this person. So then the everyday, day to day, moments belong to you or one day someone new. If you fail to do this, it can become complicated.

Still Allowing Him or Her Sex Privileges

What can I say, you have to stop it. If they call after 11:00 pm, this will result into unwanted regrets. So I could spend a lot of time and words explaining what I mean, but you get it. Stop having sex with your ex. You tell yourself it is for convenience and you have needs. In reality, it makes things complicated.

Boll Weevil is Looking for a Home

My mother used to say, "boll weevil is looking for a home" so there will be decisions made that could result in someone leaving you for another only to find out that it was better with you. So then they attempt to return not because they love you so much, but because they are looking for a home. This can be complicated if you allow your emotions to lead. Therefore, if he loves you and he wants you back, he will do what is necessary to maintain his life and relationship with you without using you. It is complicated when you won't move on emotionally and you still desire connection to a person who does not want you. It is vital to get beyond this stage because it gets complicated when you believe you love someone more than yourself. God is not the author of confusion. He desires for us to have peace that flows like a river. These complicated conditions have their roots in bad decisions. Although life can be saturated with complicated issues and circumstances, we serve a God that is a Wonderful counselor, Mighty God, Everlasting Father, Prince of Peace. (Isa 9:6) God can handle any and every condition that seems to throw us off track. However to get past these complications we must move beyond believing God and rest in KNOWING He can do it! We must make better choices. Therefore our opening Scripture comes down to a very simple thought. Say yes when you mean yes and say no when you mean no. It is important to remember not to be afraid of telling yourself no. No he can't come over when the children are sleep. No he can't contribute to your personal life choices. No he can't place demands on you that interrupt God's plans for your life. These are choices that you have to make so things will be less complicated. When you take back your emotion, take back your devotion to him or her, take back your love making, you can take back your life and move on.

However, if a bad choice is made, no worries! Just trust God to help you turn it around.

Looking to the Right Source
Chapter 12

Now unto him that is able to do exceeding abundantly above all that we ask or think, according to the power that worketh in us, Unto him be glory in the church by Christ Jesus throughout all ages, world without end. Amen.
Ephesians 3:20-21

As I look back over my life as a single mother, parent, and person, I have learned a lot. During the first few years of my singleness, I only sought to find a replacement father for my children. However God took time to show me that there was so much more that I needed. There is a Scripture in the Bible, Ephesians 3:20 says "...now to him who is able to do immeasurably more than all we ask or imagine according to his power that is at work within us, to him be glory in the church and in Christ Jesus throughout all generations, forever and ever! Amen." This text best explained where my mind needed to be. God wanted me to know that in His might, ability and will He could do anything. I only needed to learn that He is able. When we lean on our own mind, there are limitations. However when our trust is in Christ Jesus, we can overcome any limitation. We just have to trust Him. The repetitive thought in this entire book is, above all else, Trust God! He is able to do immeasurably more than what we ask or even think to ask. So, it was those limitations that God wanted to eradicate out of my life. He wanted me to know that whatever measurements that I had in my mind, He could go well beyond it because of His power. It was God's power at work in me that gave me opportunity to learn how to look and stay focused on Him. He is the right source. Throughout my litany of mistakes and bad choices, God was there to help me focus on the right source. I have become a better person because of theses better choices. Anyone that seeks a deeper relationship with God can become a better person and parent with His help. Now God has the right to quicken anything He wants us to learn. That means He can bring complete understanding in minutes. However, God can also take the approach to help you learn through the process of time. And because it is a process, it may not come overnight so we must learn to wait. Now waiting on God can be frustrating because we have preconceived ideas of how everything should work out. However, God knows the plan He has for us and His plan exposes His might, power, and authority in our lives. God has a plan to teach us that He is the right source so we always know to involve Him in times of trouble or triumph. Beloved we have to commit to memory that God, the right source, will always lead us to the way He desires for our lives. His divine detours provide us another route that leads us away from dangerous circumstances. Some things in our lives seem to repeat themselves because we fail to learn the lessons that God teaches because we get hemmed up with wrong sources. Therefore, God in His grace and mercy continues to help us learn and retain the lesson. He takes time to take us through the processes that will help us become better so we can help someone else. And that is the sole purpose of this book, to help someone get beyond getting a man and receive the mind of Christ Jesus to become a better person and parent. I see so many people that are more interested in making the person they are seeking happy instead of their children. Our children only have us to depend on. Therefore, we are responsible to lead, guide, and instruct them. Everything that we do or fail to do influences their lives for the good or bad. We are responsible to build our lives with the help of God so that when our children look at our lives they will be influenced in a positive manner. Achieving the security I wanted for myself and my children would never come through sources such as money and powerful people. God wanted me to know that the security I longed for was already mine because He was my source! God gave me the security I needed for me and my children through our inheritance through Jesus Christ. It took time to receive God's lavish investment in mankind and all of His benefits. But when I began to understand God's many blessings for me and my children, I received it and I did not look back. The text goes on to say, "...to him be glory in the church and in Christ Jesus throughout all generations for ever and ever! Amen..." So it is God's desire for us to continue to tell all generations about His glory. Therefore our children and our children's children need to know that

God loves to stand up in our lives. Our goal for our personal lives should be understanding God as the right source but also leading our children to God so that they will also know Him as the right source. When we take time to teach our children about the source they are less likely to chase resources. Beloved it is important to remember that even though there may have been events in your life that happened suddenly, God has invested His time in all His children, and that includes you! The suddenness of any circumstance can be overcome or understood with the help of God. Parenting is one of the most important tasks you will undertake in this life. However in the end it will be worth it to hear your children speak proudly of how well you did as a single parent. It will make you smile, but in your heart you will know that God led you through the process of being suddenly saved, single, and parenting! And it is God's love that will show us how to reach back and give back to someone that will one day need to know that becoming **Suddenly Saved, Single and Parenting** may have been the best thing that happened.

About the Author

Pastor Sharon Hunter is a mother, wife, business woman, author, and co-pastor of Tabernacle of Praise Christian Fellowship Church in Louisville, Kentucky with her pastor and husband Senior Pastor Dominic Hunter. They have six dynamic children and two grandchildren, Andre and Baby Kaiya Marie.

Pastor Hunter has had a relationship with God all her life. Ministry has always been Pastor Hunter's passion. She loves helping the people of God develop in their walk with God.

She has been in ministry for 18 years. She was ordained through Forest Tabernacle Baptist Church under the direction of Senior Pastor James H. Anderson Jr. in 1998. She served as the Youth minister and helped with the Women of Worship women's ministry and choir. She furthered her knowledge of church leadership while serving as Assistant to the Pastor and Church School Superintendent of Indiana Avenue Christian Church under the direction of Senior Pastor Drumondo Simpson. She also assisted with their women's ministry, choir and youth.

Currently, Pastor Hunter co-Pastors with her husband and Senior Pastor Dominic J. Hunter. She loves supporting and assisting the vison God gave Sr. Pastor D. Hunter: WE ARE KINGDOM BUILDERS WITH A KINGDOM MIND TO DO KINGDOM WORK!

Ministry is her life so she travels wherever God sends her and helps her husband in various capacities of their Church for the last 5 ½ years.

Pastor Hunter is a graduate of Indiana Wesleyan University with a Bachelor's degree in Business Administration and Management.

She also is the author of two children's books, "Sustahgirl and the Annoying Sonnyboy" and "Sustahgirl and Mystery of the Giant Hair."

Pastor Hunter believes

#Great Readers Make Great Leaders

She has a third book, "Suddenly Saved, Single and Parenting" for adults which will be released in April 2016 that will strive to help Christian women who are saved, single, and parenting overcome some of life's troublesome obstacles. Pastor Hunter is also a singer and songwriter which is another one of her ministry passions. Her goal is to impact lives through books, music and communication. She desires to help families get beyond the dream of abundant living to the actual reality of abundant living every single day!

For More information about Pastor Hunter visit: www.sustahgirl.com or
http://about.me/sharonbriggshunter

www.ingramcontent.com/pod-product-compliance
Lightning Source LLC
Chambersburg PA
CBHW051700090426
42736CB00013B/2461